Candle Making

-

Homemade Candles for beginners

By Sandra Nixon

Table of Contents

HISTORY OF CANDLE MAKING 1

    CULTURAL IMPORTANCE OF CANDLES...10

TOOLS YOU WILL NEED 14

DIFFERENT TYPES OF CANDLE WAX 18

    PARAFFIN 19

    CREAM WAX 20

    GEL WAX 21

    SOY WAX 23

    PALM WAX 25

    BAYBERRY WAX..25

    BEESWAX 27

    TALLOW WAX 28

DIFFERENT TYPES OF CANDLE WICKS... 29

    FLAT WICKS...31

    SQUARE OR ROUND WICKS 32

    CORED WICKS 33

    HTP WICK 34

    LX WICKS...35

    RRD WICKS...36

    CD WICKS 37

    MATERIALS FOR CANDLE WICKS..38

CANDLE SCENTS.. 39

CANDLE COLORS 47

THE CANDLE MAKING PROCESS 51

    MELTING 51

    ADDING SCENTS AND COLORS 52

    WICKING 52

    POURING 54

    CURING 54

    TRIMMING THE WICK 54

    FINISHING TOUCHES..55

LAYERING COLORS AND SCENTS..**56**

BASIC DIY CANDLE RECIPES **58**

TROUBLESHOOTING AND TIPS **66**

    COMMON CANDLE PROBLEMS 66
    TIPS.. 69

History of Candle Making

Do you realize human beings are using candles for thousands of years? Based on the evidence discovered in Israel, in 2008, the human race has been using fire since 790,000 years ago. The discovery of fire is the first remarkable step in the development of the human race. The history of the candle is also associated with the discovery of fire. The first candles were the torches that people used to transport fire. However, the proper candles, the candles made from wax and wick, were made 5000 years ago.

The prototypes of the candles that we know today were first made by Egyptians. They made candles by covering straw with animal fats or resin. In 3000 BC, the Egyptians were already using wicked candles. The Romans also made candles. Their candles were made from papyrus, tallow or beeswax.

Just like the human species evolving simultaneously in various regions, candle making also developed at the same time in various cultures. The Roman, the Chinese and the Indian civilization began making candles. However, candles were not used in Europe, the Middle-East, and Africa because olive oil lamps were more popular and cheaper. These cultures did not start using wax before the middle ages. In the beginning, candles were made from tallow and beeswax. Later, people began making candles from spermaceti, purified animal fats, and paraffin wax.

Candles in the Antiquity

The Romans used oil lamps for lighting purposes, however, they were already making candles around 500 BC. These candles were made from tallow. The Romans gave candles as gifts during the festival of Saturn.

The earliest evidence of candle in China dates back to the Qin Dynasty (221–206 BC). Candles made from whale fat have been found in a mausoleum of Qin Shi Huang, the first emperor of the Qin Dynasty.

A Jizhupian dictionary that dates back to 40 BC mentions about candles made of beeswax. Another ancient Chinese text, the Book of Jin dating back to 648 AD that features the Jin Dynasty (265–420 AD), mentions that beeswax candles were used by the statesman Zhou Yi.

The Chinese candles were molded in paper tubes, using rolled rice paper for the wick, and wax from an indigenous insect.
The Japanese have also been making candles since ancient times. Their candles were made from wax extracted from tree nuts.

In Tibet, yak butter was used to make candles, which is still in use. Candles were also made in India. These candles were made from the wax derived by boiling cinnamon.

During the 1st century AD, the indigenous people in Alaska made candles from fish oil, they referred the fish as candlefish.

Candles in the Middle Age

In the middle age, olive oil was the primary source of fuel for oil lamps. Olive oil lamps were used in Europe, North Africa, and the Middle East. After the Roman Empire collapsed, there was a trading disruption between Europe and North Africa and the Middle East. The trading disruption made olive oil scarce in Europe. This provided a fertile ground for candle making. Contrarily, the North Africans and Middle Eastern continued using olive oil and did not explore making candles with wax.

The Romans and the Egyptians were the early candle makers. However, the candle as we know today is actually credited to the Byzantine Empire. In the Byzantine Empire, as early as the 7th century, there were professional candle makers referred to as chandlers. The book of Eparch contains instructions on candle making like it was back in the day.

There were two kinds of candles available back then, one that was made from tallow, and two that were made from beeswax. Tallow candles gave smoke and smell. Interestingly, due to its unpleasant odor, some countries passed an ordinance that banned tallow candles. Beeswax candles were not smoky and smelly. Actually, they produced a sweet smell. Beeswax candles were expensive and beyond the reach of ordinary people, they were used by rich people. Beeswax candles were also used in worship.

By the 13th century, candles became more popular. The candle makers, or chandlers, made candles from the fat of goats, sheep or cows. Beeswax and tallow were still used. The first commercial candle making company was established in England in 1300 by the name The Tallow Chandlers Company of London, the company gained the coat of arms in 1456. London streets were being lighted by tallow candles by 1415.

Candles in the Modern Age

The birth of modern candle making is credited to the whaling industry. During the 18th century, commercial whaling began. People discovered spermaceti (a kind of oil) in the head of the sperm whale.

The source of spermaceti

The discovery of spermaceti led to the mass production of candles. Spermaceti was considered an ideal substance for candles because it did not produce smell and smoke, it burned brightly, and was also harder than beeswax or tallow, therefore did not soften during the summer. Spermaceti wax candles were the first "standard candles" available to anyone.

During the early 1800s, it was discovered that candles could also be made from the oils from the plants of Brassica species or Colza plant. This was a cheaper alternative than the spermaceti.

The colza plant

Today, candles are made from paraffin by pressing, drawing, casting, or dipping. There are hundreds of commercial candle makers in Europe and America. There are even associations of commercial or indie candle makers. The International Guild of Candle Artisans is an association of candle making companies or individual candle makers.

Industrialization of Candle Making

The industrialization of candle making is credited to the invention of the candle making machine. In 1834, an Englishman named Joseph Morgan patented a machine that manufactured 1500 candles every hour. The candle making machine revolutionized candle making. Since the mass-making of candles was possible, candles became affordable to the mass.

An old commercial candle making machine

During this time, changes were also made in the candle wicks. Until then the wicks were the twisted strands of cotton, but the makers began using braided cotton threads. The new wicks made the candle brighter.

The first oil refinery was established in 1848, in Derbyshire, England, by James Young. Crude oil contains paraffin. Making candles from paraffin became possible two years later when Young was able to refine crude oil through the distillation process.

Paraffin was the cheapest substance for candles. However, the early paraffin also had a low melting point. The problem was solved by using stearin. Most of the candles manufactured during the 19th century had paraffin and stearic acid. Stearin was discovered in 1825 by two French chemists Michel Eugène Chevreul and Joseph-Louis Gay-Lussac. This substance was derived from plants or animal fats, but unlike tallow, it did not have glycerine, so it was not smelly or smoky.

The Decline of the Candle Industry

The primary purpose of the candle was to provide light. However, with the invention and discovery of better lighting techniques, the candle industry declined. The discovery of the kerosene lamp challenged the candles, and the invention of the incandescent light bulb in 1879 knocked down the candle industry.

Electricity is a cheap source of light, even in places where electricity is not available there are better alternatives such as solar light, batteries or kerosene lamps. Therefore, candles as the primary source of light has completely been replaced.

Evolution of Decorative and Scented Candles

It is true that people are no longer using candles for lighting their homes, however, candles have not been completely wiped out from the face of the earth. People have discovered new ways of using candles such as decorative candles, colored candles, and scented candles.

These are used for various purposes such as worship, meditation, romantic dinners, setting the mood, creating an ambiance in the room, home decoration, etc. Specialized candles are becoming popular these days.

During the late 20th century, paraffin was replaced with new kinds of wax. Soy, palm and flax-seed oils were blended with paraffin to create a new wax. People also added color pigments and essential oils to the candle wax to make special candles. Currently, scented candles are trending.

The market is still growing. Not only companies but also the people are producing scented candles themselves.

Cultural Importance of Candles

Christmas Candles

If you are a Christian, you must be already aware of candle traditions. The candle is a very important aspect of Christian worshipping and Christian celebrations. Lighting candles in the Church or during Christmas are popular traditions. What you might not be aware of is that the lighting candle is not an original Christian tradition. In the ancient time, people used to light candles during winter solstice celebrations, which was a way of remembering that the spring would soon come. Christians could have taken over that tradition.

The earliest records of candles being used at Christmas belongs to the middle ages. A large candle was used to represent the star of Bethlehem. Jesus is referred to as 'the Light of the World.' And this could have also started the custom of the Advent Candles. Before the electrical lights were invented, candles were also used to decorate the Christmas tree.

Side note: If you don't want your house the be a giant candle, don't put them in your Christmas tree!

Hanukkiah Candles

If you belong to the Jewish culture, you might already know how important candles are. Hanukkiah is a Jewish festival of light, during which it is very common to light candles. A candle is lit on a branched candlestick called a 'hanukkiah' for the eight nights of Hanukkiah. The history of Hanukkah goes back to 165 BC. Can you imagine how long the Jewish people have been lighting candles?

Diwali Candles

Candles are also important in Hindu culture. Diwali is the Hindu festival of light. Lighting candles is a popular tradition during Diwali. To mark Diwali, the Hindus decorate their houses and garden with candles. This tradition is now being replaced with electric lights.

Wedding Candles

If you had a Christian marriage or participated in the wedding function in a church, you might have noticed the tradition of the unity candle. Lighting a unity candle is a common Christian wedding ritual.

Christian marriage begins with the lighting of two taper candles by the representative of the bride and the groom (usually the mothers). After the marriage vows are taken, the bride and groom light the unity candle together from the candles lit by their mothers.

The lighting of taper candles and the unity candles are symbolized as the unity of two families and the union of a man and a woman. Interestingly, many people believe that this is a recent tradition.

A unity Candle

Tools You Will Need

Whether you want to make candles for your personal use or make a profit by selling candles, the first question that will pop up in your mind is: What kind of candle making supplies do I need?

Let's get started. You will need the following things:

Wax: Wax is the basic ingredient in a candle. There are different kinds of wax available. What kinds of wax you need depends on the type of candle you are going to make.

Wicks: Wicks is the second most important thing to have in the candle making process. You need a wick to light the candle. If you do not use a good wick, your candle will not burn properly. You can choose a variety of wicks. The performance of your candle depends on the type of wick you use.

Fragrance oil: If you are making simple candles, you do not require fragrance oil, however, if you want to make scented candles, you need fragrance oil. You can choose a variety of fragrance oils for your candle. The recommended amount of fragrance is 1 ounce of fragrance oil in 16 ounces (1 pound) of wax. You can make your own preferred mixing ratio too.

Color: You need color pigment to make colorful candles. You can choose between dye chips, blocks or liquid dye.

Containers: You need containers or molds to give a shape to your candles. You can choose a variety of candle containers such as a tin container, glass container, etc.

Scale: You need a scale to measure wax, fragrance oil, and color.

Stove: In order to make a candle, you should first start with melting the wax. You need a stove for that purpose.

Saucepans or pitcher: You need a saucepan or a pitcher to melt the wax. Instead of direct melting, many people prefer to melt wax indirectly. Indirect melting is done by boiling water in the saucepan and placing the pitcher with wax over the boiling water.

A safe way of melting wax: "the double boiler"

Thermometer: As the wax begins to melt, you need to measure the temperature. Therefore, you need a thermometer. Don't use one with plastic on it!

Candle labels: If the primary purpose of making candles is to profit by selling candles, you need a label. The label should include details of the manufacturer and safety measures.

Miscellaneous items: You also need disposable latex gloves, old newspapers to cover your working table, paper towels, alcohol to clean your containers, and candle boxes to store your candles.

Different types of candle wax

Now that you know how candles were made back in the day and what you need to make candles, let's get started with candle making. The first step in making a candle is to understand the candle wax.

Wax and wicks are two major ingredients for a candle, the rest of the things are just additives to make specialized candles. There are different kinds of candle wax. The kind of wax you choose depends on the type of candle you want to make. The candle wax determines various things such as melting points and reaction to the additives like fragrance and color.

Different types of wax have different melting points. Generally speaking, soft wax has a low melting point and hard wax has a high melting point. While buying candle wax, you should always check the type of wax, the melting point, and the reaction to the additives (if any).

Here are some common waxes used for candle making.

Paraffin

Paraffin is the most common candle wax. It is also the cheapest wax available on the market. Paraffin is derived during the refining of petroleum. If you are just beginning to make candles, you should work with paraffin. Making candles from paraffin will teach you a lot about how to make candles. The melting point for paraffin wax has a wide variation. Paraffin has low, moderate as well as high melting points. Because of this variation, you can make various types of candles from paraffin.

You can also use paraffin wax to make candles with snowflakes effects and crystal patterns. Paraffin gives you a kind of flexibility that no other wax will give you.

Pros

- Paraffin is the cheapest candle wax. Therefore, you can make many candles on a small budget.
- Paraffin is the best candle wax for beginners.
- You can make decorative candles from paraffin.
- You can use any type of candle dyes.
- You can use any kind of candle fragrance.
- You can use any kind of additives.

Cons

- Paraffin is not environmentally friendly as it is derived from oil mining.
- Paraffin is non-biodegrade.

Cream Wax

Paraffin does not contain natural oils, however, when paraffin is mixed with natural oils, the wax we get is cream wax. Cream wax contains mineral oil and resin compounds. Cream wax is clean. It burns consistently, without any interruptions such as bubbles. It has a high melting point, therefore, there will be no soot left (black ash against the glass jar).

Cream wax is solid, yet soft. If you want to make scented candles, cream wax is better than paraffin wax. Cream wax makes the best container candles. Sadly, you cannot make a tapered candle with cream wax.

Pros

- Cream wax is the best option for a container candle.
- Cream wax is good for beginners.

Cons
- It can be used only for container-based candles.

Gel Wax

Gel wax is derived from mineral oils. Normally, gel wax is used for themed candles. It is clear and even if you use dyes, it remains see-through. Gel wax is also odorless.

You can embed various decorative objects – for instance, a glass fish or glitters – in a gel candle. Gel wax has an opaque appearance and does not easily mix with additives. Gel wax has a high melting point.

Gel wax is different from paraffin wax or vegetable wax. Interestingly, you cannot make tapered candles with gel wax; you have to pour the gel wax in a container to make candles. If you want to use scents, you have to choose fragrance wisely because gel wax does not support all kinds of fragrance oils.

Since gel wax has a high melting point, it generates high temperatures. If you are using a thin glass container for gel wax, your container might crack.

Pros

- Gel wax is the ideal choice for decorative candles.
- You can use gel wax to make candles with various designs like glitters, floating beads, underwater scenes, etc.
- You can make a collectible candle from gel wax.
- Gel candles burn slowly, making your candle last longer.
- Gel wax candles are easier to handle.

Cons

- You cannot use cotton wicks because cotton does not burn well in gel candles.
- You need to choose the container for the gel candle wisely as it might crack.
- Gel wax candles create bubbles while burning.

Soy Wax

Soy is a highly beneficial plant. It is the ultimate protein source for vegetarians and vegans. Soy can be used in many ways. You can not only use soybeans as food but also make milk, tofu, oil, and wax as well.

Using soy for a candle is quite a recent discovery. When soybean oil is hydrogenated, we get soy wax. Since soy wax comes from soybean oil, it has natural oils, thus it blends very well with natural additives and natural fragrance oils. Soy wax has different melting points which differ according to the additives used. You can use soy wax to make a variety of candles.

Pros

- It is comparatively inexpensive.
- The wax burns clearly.
- Since soy is plant-based wax, unlike paraffin, soy wax is a sustainable resource.
- Good for the environment because unlike paraffin it does not do any environmental damages.
- Soy wax is biodegradable.
- It is easy to clean soy wax when it spills on something, no carcinogenic chemical is required.
- The best wax to make large candles.

Cons

- It is hard to mix some chemical fragrance oils with soy wax because soybean oil does not hold all types of oil.
- Soy wax does not easily hold dyes, therefore, you need to find dyes especially made for soy wax.
- Making candles from soy wax is not for beginners.
- Soy wax burns faster.

Palm Wax

Palm wax is a plant-based wax; it is derived from palm trees. Palm wax has a long burning time, the longest from all of the plant-based wax. Palm wax produces a bright flame, much brighter than most of the other waxes. Palm wax candles do not produce smoke. It has a high melting point, therefore, it is best used in hot climates.

Pros
- Since palm wax is plant-based wax, it does not harm the environment.
- It is biodegradable, thus, it is environment-friendly.
- Best candle wax for long-lasting candles.

Cons
- Very expensive.
- It can be very challenging to work with.

Bayberry Wax

The fruits of the bayberry plant are naturally coated with wax. Also called candleberry, the bayberry wax is derived by boiling the berries from this plant. When bayberries are boiled, wax collects on the top, it is then scraped and collected. The bayberry wax has green pigmentation, therefore, you do not have to use green dyes if you want to make green candles. The wax has a sweet, floral smell, thus, it is ideal for making scented candles.

Comparatively, bayberry wax is expensive. One of the reasons why the bayberry wax is expensive is because it takes a lot of time to make wax from bayberries. They are generally used during special occasions like Christmas and New Year.

Pros

- Traditionally, the bayberry candles are thought to bring fortune and prosperity.
- It has a natural aroma.
- Environmentally friendly, as it comes from natural sources.

Cons

- The bayberry wax has to be mixed with other plant-based wax in order to make strong bayberry candles, usually beeswax.
- This is an expensive option for candle wax.

Beeswax

As the name suggests, beeswax is made by honeybees. It is found in honeycombs. Beeswax is yellow or brown in color and has a sweet smell. The wax burns slower and releases aroma as it burns. Beeswax has a high melting point.

Pros
- Has a natural aroma
- Burns slow
- Gives white light instead of yellow flame.
- environment-friendly.
- Ideal candle wax for making hand-sculpted candles.

Cons
- Due to the presence of honey; scent and fragrance oils do not easily mix with beeswax.
- More on the expensive side

- Due to its sticky nature, cleaning can be difficult in case it spills on the carpet or clothes.

Tallow Wax

The first proper candles, the candles made from wax and wick, were made from tallow wax. Tallow is the wax derived from animal fat. Fat from domestic animals such as sheep, pigs, and cattle was used as candle wax for a long time until spermaceti was discovered in the 18th century and paraffin in the 19th century. Actually, Spermaceti is also animal-based fat, however, unlike tallow, Spermaceti does not give smoke or odor while burning.

Tallow wax does not have color and has a low melting point

Pros
- People made candles from tallow for hundreds of years.

Cons
- Emits smoke while burning
- Gives a bad odor when burned.

Different types of candle wicks

The wick is a very important part of a candle. Generally speaking, without a wick, there will be no candle. The candle burns from the wick and the wick act as an intermediary between the flame and wax. It provides fuel to the flame. The wick absorbs the fuel and sends it to the flame, and then vaporizes and burns.

The wick used in the candle influences the candlelight. For the candle to burn bright, thickness, strength, tethering, and fire-resistance, all are important. Braided cotton is the common wick for candles, however, other materials are also used as a candle wick, for instance, wood or metal. People also use tampons as a wick while making impromptu candles.

When the wicks are thick in diameter, it melts more wax, thus generating a brighter flame. Thick wax also burns the candle faster. These days, flat braided wicks are common. Flat braided wick twirls as they burn, which makes them self-consuming.

In a container candle, the wick is fixed on the bottom of the container so that it does not float on the melted wax.

Sometimes stiffeners such as fine copper wire, synthetic fibers, or papers are used with the wick to give it strength. Metal stiffeners also work as the heat conductor. Stiffeners are generally used in the hard candle wax.

The candle wick has to be treated with fire-resistant solutions before it is used in the candle. When the wick is not treated with fire-resistant solutions, the wick will easily die due to the heat generated during the burning of candles. Wicks are also treated with various substances in order to improve the brightness and the color of the flame. Treatment also provides strength to the wick. The common wick treatment solvents are salt and borax.

If you are a new candle maker, you might be overwhelmed with the available sizes and types of wicks. You should choose a wick wisely because the wick determines how the candle burns. Before you get started with candle making, you need to understand the shape, size, and material of the wick.
Generally speaking, there are four major types of wicks.

Flat wicks

Flat wicks are the most common type of candlewick. Flat wicks are used in pillar and taper candles. Three strings of fiber are plaited or knitted to make flat wicks. These wicks curl while burning, thus giving the consistent light through self-trimming effect without producing too much of a black tip.

Since flat braid wicks are constructed from 100% natural fibers, manufacturers usually add some chemical treatment to improve its burn performance. Due to this reason, flat braid wicks are ideal in paraffin based waxes.

Square or Round Wicks

Square wicks are also knitted or plaited and they curl while burning. The only difference between square wicks and flat wicks is square wicks are rounded whereas flat wicks are flat. Square wicks are stronger and thicker than the flat wicks. Since these wicks are thicker, there are no possibilities of wick clogging. Square wicks are generally used for beeswax candles.

Cored Wicks

These kinds of wicks are the most used in candle making. Flat wicks and square wicks are stand-alone wicks; however, cored wicks use a core material for support.

Core wicks are also braided, but they need paper, cotton, zinc, or tin as support. The core material is used for the stiffness. Cored wicks are generally found in container candles like devotional candles, jar candles, and pillar candles.

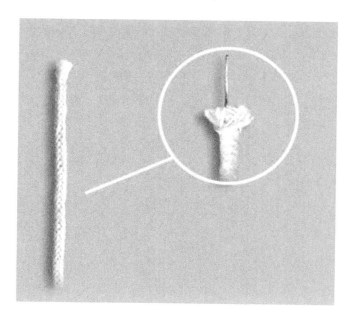

HTP wick

Another type of wick that is very popular in candle making projects is the HTP wick. Made from a combination of cotton flat braids and paper filaments, this type of wick offers a self-trimming characteristic coupled with the structural strength found in paper core wicks.

The added rigidity offered by these wicks is due to the high-quality stitching of the braids that improve the wax pool symmetry while reducing carbon build-up commonly known as mushrooming. Due to their excellent characteristics, HTP wicks are highly used in most natural waxes (such as soy wax), vegetable waxes and low melting point waxes (such as paraffin wax).

LX wicks

Another type of wick we're going to review here is the LX wick. A flat braided wick with stabilizing threads, the LX wick is also referred to as a coreless wick due to the omission of a metal (zinc) core. LX wicks are designed with a very solid wick construction that offers a stable, consistent and bright flame with minimized carbon, soot and afterglow rate.

With the ability to produce hot flames, LX wicks are highly usable in gel wax and crystal wax and are the best for improving burn rate in paraffin wax and soy wax.

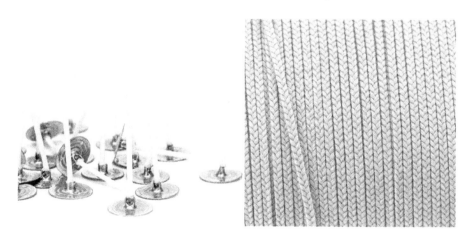

RRD wicks

The RRD wick is another popular type of wick used in most candle making projects. Quite similar to the LX wick, the RRD wick is stitched from cotton core braids and tension threads to give it a steady and more reinforced characteristic when burning. Due to the strength of the wick, RRD wicks are mostly used in container candles, vegetable-based waxes, soy wax, gel wax, solid scented and solid-colored votive candles.

Just like other wicks, RRD wicks are designed to curl at the top to produce a hotter burn with less smoke and less carbon build-up. In addition to that, these wicks are self-trimming making them the best choice for most candle making projects. RRD wicks are made from 100% cotton core dipped in natural wax for efficient burning. These wicks produce a nice even burn and are highly used in most candle making projects.

CD wicks

Finally, we have the CD wicks. Also referred to as coreless wicks (since they don't have a metal core), these wicks are interwoven with paper threads in flat braid style to make them steady with improved rigidity. Although these wicks are not designed with zinc metals (which burns hot), the flat braid paper design—with improved burn rate—makes these wicks the best for harder-to-melt waxes such as soy wax, paraffin wax, and vegetable-based waxes.

Finally, CD wicks are designed with a curved tip to improve burning and make them self-trimming with reduced soot and mushrooming. CD wicks are mostly preferred by hobbyists and can be purchased either in raw form or pre-waxed.

Materials for candle wicks

About 80 percent of candle wicks are made from cotton or the combination of cotton and paper, the rest of the wick is metal- and paper-cored wicks. Candle wicks are braided cotton threads in different dimensions. The wicks that are coated with wax are used with oil-based waxes. However, if you are using gel wax, wicks should not be coated with wax as it can cloud the gel.

There was a time when lead was also used in candle wicks, however, this is banned in the US and many other countries. The cored wicks, which are generally used in container candles, make use of zinc or tin.

When you are making candles, you can buy ready to be used wicks or make your own wicks. Basically, candle wicks are made in three ways:

- Borax candle wick
- Wooden candle wick
- Moveable candle wick

One of the easiest ways to make candle wick is by dipping braided cotton thread in melted wax. How candle wicks are made will be explained in the following chapter.

Candle Scents

In the late 20th century, people discovered a new type of wax by blending palm oil, flax-seed oil and soy oil with paraffin wax. These new waxes gave fragrance while burning. Thus began the search for scented candles. Candlemakers add synthetic fragrance, fragrance oils, essential oils, and scented herbs to create scented candles.

Today, scented candles have such a huge market share that about 80 percent of the candles sold in the United States are scented candles. Candlemakers are constantly working with fragrance companies to develop new candles. These days you can find candles of various scents from garden spices to exotic herbs, fruits, flowers, you name it. Scented candles are made by infusing essential oils, fragrance oils and scented herbs in candle wax.

When you burn a normal candle, it will produce water vapor and carbon dioxide. likewise, when you burn a scented candle, in addition to water vapor and carbon dioxide, it will also release aroma in the air. The aroma is released through evaporation of fragrance from the melted wax.

Generally speaking, two kinds of fragrances are used in candles: natural fragrance and synthetic fragrance. Natural fragrances are derived from essential oils and scented herbs. Synthetic fragrances are chemical-based fragrance.
Not all kinds of fragrances work with all kinds of candle waxes. In order to ensure that the candle burns properly, a good formulation of candle wax and candle fragrance should be used.

You can find over 2000 natural and chemical fragrances that can be used in candles as well as cosmetics, perfumes, lotions, shampoo and bath soaps.

You can use scented candles to remove odor and have a sweet aroma in your house or set the ambiance or mood. It is more natural to burn scented candles than spray a room freshener. It is also more convenient to light scented candles than burn essential oils in the aroma burner.

While making candles, you can use any kind of fragrance oils, essential oils, scented herbs or synthetic fragrances, however, you need to check whether these additives are compatible with the wax you are using. Some fragrance oils blend well, whereas others don't.

If you want to have a strong scent, you have to use more fragrance oils. While using essential oils, you also need to check out whether this particular fragrance oil will work on the wax you are using for candles. If the oil does not work with the wax, your candle will not burn properly. You must also be aware that some essential oils require thicker wicks.

How do you add scented oils, essential oils or fragrance oils in wax to create scented candles? This is not as complicated as it sounds. Melt the wax and then add fragrance oil. Stir the solution and pour it into your mold or jar.

Measurement is very important to create good fragrances. Therefore, you need to measure the wax and add essential oils in the recommended quantity that's described on the label.

Melting wax is also important. It is easy to melt soy wax, all you have to do is measure the wax and keep the container in the microwave. However, if you are using paraffin wax or beeswax, you need a double boiler. The general rule of thumb is to use 25-30 drops essential oils in one ounce of wax (one ounce of essential oil per pound of wax).

If you want to add scented herbs on your candle how do you do it? Well, the process is not so complicated actually. You will have to press herbs with wax during the candle making process. The herbal scent will be released as the melting wax heats the herbs while the candle burns.

Here are some of the common essential oils, fragrance oils and scented herbs that you can use with your candles to make scented candles.

Patchouli essential oil: Patchouli is a small East Indian shrubby mint. The leaves are highly aromatic. The essential oil from the patchouli plant is used to create a fragrance in various things, including candles. You can add patchouli oil on candles to create an earthy aroma. Alternatively, you can also blend patchouli oil with other essential oils to create a distinct aroma.

Juniper berry essential oil: The essential oil derived from juniper berries have a mild fragrance. You can use this as a standalone fragrance for your candles as well as mix with other fragrance oils.

Peppermint essential oil: Peppermint essential oil has a fresh, minty scent. The candles with peppermint smell are very popular, however, you can create unique scent by blending peppermint essential oil with other mints, spearmint for instance, or floral fragrance oils.

Cinnamon essential oil: You get spicy, fresh smell from cinnamon essential oils. You can experiment with the scent by adding other essential oils. Try mixing orange essential oil with cinnamon essential oils to make a spicy-citrus smell.

Jasmine essential oil: If you like the floral smell, you should try adding jasmine essential oil in your candles. Jasmine essential oil blends well with other floral oils or herbal oil. You can use jasmine essential oil along with bergamot essential oil, orange oil, and cedarwood.

Lavender essential oil: Lavender is a highly aromatic flower. Lavender essential oil has numerous health benefits. It not only relieves you from stress and boosts your mood, but also helps in getting a good sleep. You can try lavender with other essential oils. Sage oil blends perfectly with lavender oil.

Eucalyptus essential oil: You can either use eucalyptus essential oils in your candle to create woody eucalyptus fragrance or blend eucalyptus oil with other oil, peppermint for instance or create a woody fragrance with a minty touch. By the way, candles created from eucalyptus oil and peppermint oil have decongestant properties.

Palmarosa essential oil: Palmarosa essential oil is a cheap alternative to rose oil because Palmarosa essential oil just smells like a rose. The best thing about this essential oil is that the fragrance lasts long. You can mix Palmarosa essential oil with other floral oils or even cedarwood oil or sandalwood oil to create a woody smell with floral twang.

Myrrh essential oil: Myrrh is highly aromatic. It is used in perfumes, bath soaps, and cosmetics. Myrrh well with other essential oils. Try blending myrrh with juniper berry oil, cypress oil, sandalwood oil, or even peppermint oil.

Chocolate: People love chocolates. You can easily create chocolate scented candles by using chocolate scented synthetic fragrance oil. You can mix this oil with other fragrances to create unique scents. If you are confused about the kind of chocolate scent for your candles, try mint chocolate.

Fresh laundry: Do you like the smell of your fresh laundry? If yes, you can find synthetic fragrance oils that give a scent just like freshly washed clothes.

Lemon-scented candles: Many people love the citrus smell of lemon. Therefore, lemon-scented candles are very popular. However, the general practice of making candles with lemon scents is by pairing the lemon scent with other fragrances. Lemon-scented candles can be used as a room freshener because the smell is long-lasting.

Sandalwood: Sandalwood is a popular scent for candles, perfumes, bath soaps, cosmetics, etc. Some people find sandalwood smelling a little muskier, therefore, candle makers prefer to blend sandalwood with jasmine or patchouli.

Apple scent: Many people love the smell of apples, therefore apple scented candles are very popular. If you want mild aroma, apple scented candles are best. The common practice of making apple scented candles is by mixing apple scent with a cinnamon smell.

Rose oil: Rose is a highly aromatic flower. Rose oil and rose fragrance oils are commonly used in perfumes and cosmetics. You can use rose essential oils or synthetic rose fragrance to create rose-scented candles.

Coconut oil: Coconut oils are commonly mixed with soy wax, beeswax, or paraffin wax to create candle wax that gives coconut scent. Coconut scented candles give you a feel of the tropical atmosphere.

Vanilla scent: Vanilla is a popular scent. You can either use vanilla extracts or synthetic fragrance to create vanilla scented candles. Vanilla is so versatile that it blends well with other fragrances thus creating a unique scent.

These are just a few examples of the fragrances that you can use on your candles to create scented candles. You can also try basil, sage, lemongrass, Ylang Ylang, vetiver, and anise; the options are unlimited.

Candle Colors

Gone are the days when candles were used only for lighting. Today, candles are used for decorative purposes. Since candles are used to set up the ambiance, boost mood, and create aroma when burned, candles are made with various colors. Candles are available in the common ivory shade to the rich jewel tones, metallic color or chromatic layers.

Today, the fragrance is the most important factor in the candle business and color is the second important factor that determines the candle sales. Consumers choose candles based on the fragrance and color they like. The choice for color is based on the psychology of the consumer. Generally speaking, the consumers associate the fragrance of the candle with the color of the candle.

The beauty of candle lies in the design and color. Therefore, you should be very careful about choosing the right color for your candles. The color of your candle is affected by the type of coloring agent and the amount of coloring agent you have used. How well the color will produce is also determined by the type of candle wax you are using.

There are two main options for making colored candles: Dyes and Pigments. While making colored candles, you will be using dyes and pigments in different ways because these coloring agents create different color effects. Dyes are basically used to color the entire candle whereas pigments are used to add color to the candle surface.

Pigments and dyes are both safe. No health hazards have been discovered so far.

Types of Candle Dyes

There are four different types of dyes available for the candle makers. Your choice of dye should depend on the money you want to spend and the number of candles you want to make. The four candle dyes are dye blocks, powder dyes, liquid dyes, and dye chips.

Candle Dye Blocks: Blocks are the cheapest colorants for candles. Generally speaking, you can color 5-pounds of candle wax with one dye block.

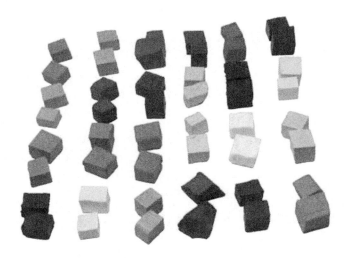

Powdered Candle Dye: If you want to use a powdered candle dye, you have few color options to choose from. Powder candle dye is highly concentrated and very useful while coloring many candles.

Liquid Candle Dye: Liquid candle dye can get messy if not handled properly. You have to use a dropper and use 4-8 drops for each pound of wax.

Candle Dye Chips: You get the precise color if you use candle dye chips. The recommended use of candle dye chips is one chip per pound of wax. If you are making a small number of candles, chips are very useful.

Don't use crayons

Can I use crayons to color my candles? This is one of the most common questions asked by most armature or beginner candle makers. Although crayons deliver wonderful vibrant colors during art and craft projects, that's not the case when it comes to candle dying. The reason behind this is due to the actual colorant used in crayons. Crayons are colored by pigments and as you all know; pigments are not soluble in wax.

Now, when crayons are heated, they break down into small pigments that tend to disperse or rather float around the molten wax instead of dissolving. Although they may appear to have changed the color of the wax, these pigments affect the burning rate of the wick making the candle poor quality. What really happens is that the pigments are sucked together with wax during burning but unfortunately, they tend to clog the wick thus preventing your candles from burning properly. Peppermint and spirulina are other colors that can be used to color your candles. However, just like crayons, these types of colors are not soluble to wax making them easier to clog the wick or settle at the bottom of a candle just like pigments.

So in summary, avoid using crayons when coloring your candles and only stick to dyes formulated for candle making projects to avoid compromising with the overall quality of your candles.

The candle making process

Melting

The candle making begins with melting wax. You can melt the candle wax in various ways. One of the easiest ways to melt wax is by putting wax in a cup and then heating it in the microwave. However, not all kinds of wax can be heated this way. The wax such as soy wax that has a low melting point can be heated in a microwave.

You can melt wax in a double boiler. However, if you do not have a double boiler, you can create your own. Place a saucepan on the stove, pour water and bring it to simmer. Put wax in a container and place it in the saucepan. As the water in the saucepan heats up, the wax inside the container gradually melts. It's like melting chocolate: putting the chocolate directly in the saucepan will burn it. That's why people use double boilers.

Different waxes require different temperatures to reach a melting point. Paraffin has the lowest melting point which ranges between 122−140°F (50−60°C) followed by beeswax which melts at 145−175°F (62.7−79.4°C) then soy wax with the highest melting point of 170−180°F (76.6−82.2°C). You should check the label on the package to be sure.

Adding Scents and Colors

If you are making colored candles or scented candles, you will have to add colorants and scents after the wax is melted. You will have to stir properly.

In the next chapter, we will talk more about scents and color layering.

Wicking

If you don't want to buy candle wicks and want to make your own wicks, the easiest way is by dipping cotton thread in the melted wax. In case you want to try the elaborate wick making methods, you can try Borax Candle Wicks, Wooden Candle Wicks, or Moveable Candle Wicks.

Borax Candle Wicks

Borax treated wick burns brighter and burns for a longer period. Borax candlewick also produces less smoke and ash. Here's how you can make borax candlewick.

1. Heat one cup of water and let it simmer.
2. Pour the water into a bowl and add 1 tablespoon salt and 3 tablespoon borax and stir. Let the mixture dissolve.
3. Soak the braided cotton thread that you want to use as a wick in the mixture for 24 hours.
4. After 24 hours, pull the thread from the solution and let it dry for 2-3 days.
5. Melt the wax and dip the thread in the melted wax.

Borax treated wick does not require wax dipping, however, if you dip the wicks in hot wax, your wick will become stiffer and easier to handle.

When the thread dries, you can use it as a wick.

Wooden Candle Wicks

For wooden candle wicks, you need wooden strips of balsa wood. You should trim down the wick to one inch taller than the container you are using for your candle. The recommended diameter of a wooden stick that you are using a wick is between half to one and a half inches. Using wood as a candle wick gives a natural wooden scent to the candle.

1. Soak the balsa wood strip in the olive oil for 20-60 minutes. Soaking for longer duration means, the wood will absorb more oil, thus making the flame brighter. The balsa wood burns on its own, however soaking in olive oil will make it easier to catch fire.

2. Place the stick on the paper towel and let it absorb excess oil from the stick. Let the paper towel soak excess oil for 5-10 minutes.

3. Attach the stick to the container; you can use glue or a metal tab.

4. You can now pour melted wax into the container and finish your candle.

Pouring

When you are making candles, you will have to first melt the wax. When the wax is melted, you will have to add candle dye and scents (in case you want to make colored/scented candles), then after, you will have to pour the mixture in the molds or the candle containers. You can use various kinds of molds and containers for your candle.

A lot of care should be taken while pouring the melted wax because this is where accidents can occur.

Use the right equipment while pouring. Wear heat resistant gloves and an apron. Spread a sheet of paper on your working desk, and use tools to hold containers.

Curing

It does not take too long to solidify the wax, however, it takes quite long for the wax to harden. There are two basic ways of candle curing. Either you let it harden on its own by storing in a cool place for 2-3 days, or put in the fridge for 2-3 hours and let it harden.

Trimming the wick

Wick determines the burn ratio of the candle. Therefore, you need to trim the wicks before your candles are ready to use. You will have to leave at least a half-inch wick for tapered candles whereas around one inch for a container candle. Use a scissor to trim the wick.

Finishing touches

If your primary purpose of making candles is to sell candles for profit or give it to your friends and families, you will have to add a label on your candles and place it inside a box. However, if your candles are for yourself, there is no need to have a label, however, you need a box for the proper storage of your candles.

Layering colors and scents

Since we had already layered out the supplies for the jar candle recipe, we're going to commence the candle making procedure right away. to begin, plan on how many layers of colors you intend the jar candle to contain. In most cases, three layers of colors appear to be much better.

Using a weighing scale, determine the amount of soy wax you'll need for the first layer. For me, about 8 oz of wax will be enough for each layer. In our situation here, we will be making a layered colored with three varying shades of blue –

dark blue at the bottom, medium blue at the center, and light blue at the top.

Melt the wax for about two minutes before adding fragrance oil about 8 drops of blue liquid candle dye. Stir it thoroughly then set it aside to cool. Warm your jar gently while allowing the wax to cool to about 130°F. Pour the first layer gently and be careful not to spill on the walls of the jar. Allow the wax to cool for about 50 minutes before adding the second layer.

Repeat the procedure for the second layer only that this time you'll add about 5 drops of blue liquid candle dye. In this second layer, pour the wax when its 10 degrees hotter than the bottom layer. In our case, the bottom layer was 130 degrees so the medium layer should be exactly 140 degrees.

Finally, repeat the same procedure for the third layer only that this time you'll add 3 drops of blue liquid candle dye. Add fragrance oil and allow stir the wax thoroughly. Like me mentioned earlier, pour the wax with a 10 degrees' difference so you'll pour at 150 degrees. Leave the wax to cool down for an entire night before trimming the wick to about ¼ inch.

If you don't want to layer your colors horizontally you can experiment with different angles of pouring the wax into your jar. For example, holding a jar under different inclines will produce the following result:

Basic DIY candle recipes

Stress and insomnia buster candles

Things you need
- Essential oils: Rose essential oil, Ylang-Ylang essential oil, and lavender essential oil
- Soy wax
- Candle container, candlewick (cored), cups, wooden spoon, plastic wrap, etc.

Method
1. Mix 1 drop of rose essential oil, 3 drops of Ylang-Ylang essential oil, and 3 drops of lavender essential oil.
2. Take three tablespoons of soy wax and put in a cup. Cover the cup with a plastic wrap and put it into the microwave for 10 to 15 seconds. Take the cup out, stir the wax with the wooden spoon and put inside microwave again for 10 seconds. Repeat this process several times until the wax is melted.
3. Now pour the essential oils in the melted wax and stir with the wooden spoon.
4. Fix a wick on the bottom of the candle container. Pour the mixture of wax and essential oils.
5. Let the wax cool down for 10 minutes and then place the candle in the fridge for a couple of hours.
6. When you burn the candle; fragrance will slowly release. This fragrance will help you get de-stressed.

Candles for flu, headache and nasal congestion

Things you need
- Essential oils: Clary Sage essential oil, Star Anise essential oil, and Peppermint essential oil
- Soy wax
- Candle container
- Candlewick (cored)
- Wooden spoon etc.

Method
1. Add 2 drops of Clary Sage essential oil, 5 drops of Star Anise essential oil, and 5 drops of Peppermint essential oil in a cup and mix the oils properly.
2. Heat 3 tablespoons of Soy wax in a microwave. When the wax is melted, add the essential oils and stir with a wooden spoon.
3. Fix a wick in the candle container and pour the mixture of wax and essential oils. When the wax hardens, your candle is ready. You will be relieved from flu, headache and nasal congestion when you burn this candle.

Insect repellant candles

Things you need:
- Lavender essential oil, Geranium essential oil, and Lemongrass essential oil
- Soy wax
- Candle jar
- Candlewick (cored)
- Plastic wrap, cups, wooden spoon, etc.

Method
1. Add 5 drops of Lemongrass essential oil, 10 drops of Lavender essential oil, and 5 drops of Geranium essential oil in a cup and blend the oils.
2. Put 3 tablespoons of Soy wax in a cup and put inside a microwave until it melts. Add essential oils to the melted wax. Fix wick in a candle container and pour wax. When the candle cools down, place it in the fridge for two hours in order to harden the wax. Your insect repellent candle is ready.

Swirl Candles

Swirl candles have swirl color patterns. In order to make swirl candles, you need a mold or jar, a cored wick is preferred, paraffin wax, and blue dye.

A swirl candle for sale on Etsy

Start with melting paraffin wax. Secure the wick to the bottom of the jar with some melted wax.

Put some liquid blue dye at the bottom of the container. Melt the wax and add fragrance oils if needed. If not, pour the wax slowly into the container. When it's filled, take a straw or wooden stick and create a swirling motion from the bottom to the top of the jar. Do this as much as you like.

If you are pleased with the outlook, let it sit to cool. One of the interesting features of the swirl candle is every candle you make will have a unique design.

Marbled Pillar Candle

Marbled pillar candles are the candles that have marble patterns. You can easily give a marble look to your candle.

Start with melting the wax. When the wax melts properly, pour it into a loaf pan. Wait until the wax forms a thin film on the surface. This usually takes 2 minutes.

Now, take a spoon and scrape the sides of the pan. Stir the wax until it becomes thick. Add 3 drops of liquid dye to the wax and mix it slightly. Use green dye.

Pour this mixture into a wick secured pillar mold. Since the wax is thick, it does not pour easily. You will have to tap the bottom of the mold on your working table. Heat the mold's outer surface with a heat gun so that wax gets settled inside. You can also tap the mold from the top to let the wax get inside.

When the candle is cooling, make some relief holes. Now let the candle dry. Trim the wick. Your marbled pillar candle is ready.

Embedded Herbs Candle

If you want to know how to make herb embedded candles, here is easy to follow guide.

For this project, you need a light-colored taper candle, a glass jar, dried herbs or flowers, and translucent or light-colored wax. Essential oils are optional.

Place the wick on the bottom of the container. Pour some melted wax into the jar and place your herbs into the layer of wax so they will not float when filling the rest of the container.

If the layer of wax is hard, you can pour the rest of the container full with wax.

Rainbow Pillars

For this project, you need a mold, paraffin wax, and liquid dyes (yellow, orange, red, pink and blue) and a hot water bath.

Secure your wick in a container. Now divide your wax into 5 equal parts as we are going to use 5 different colors. Melt the first wax batch in a microwave or double boiler and the color. Pour the first color into the mold and start melting the second one. Once the first layer is hardened pour the second one. You can do this as many times as you would like.

To get the candle out of the mold; you need to place it in a hot water bath in order to make the sides some loose. Gently tap the candle and it will be released from the mold.

Troubleshooting and Tips

Common Candle Problems

When you are making candles, you will experience different kinds of problems. While it is impossible to address each and every problem that you might encounter, we have provided reasons for some common candle problems and how you can solve them.

Flame is small or drowns on the melted wax
Reason: The wick is too thin or the wax is too hard for the wick.
Solution: Use a thick wick or soft wax. If you are using wax hardening additive, avoid using it or reduce the amount.

Wick creates excessive smoke or soot
Reasons: Wax might contain too many additives like dyes, fragrance, etc., or the wick is too thick.
Solution: Use little additives or use a thin wick.

The flame is too big
Reason: Wick used in the candles might be too big.
Solution: Use a small-sized wick or trim the wick to a half-inch.

Color fades quick
Reason: Candles might have been exposed to hard light, or a low-quality dye and wax have been used.

Solution: Store candles in a dark area to prevent direct sunlight. Add UV inhibitor to the candle wax, use good quality dye and wax.

Candles give little or no scent
Reason: Fragrance was added too quickly, too little fragrance was used, the fragrance oil was low quality or the wax was low quality.
Solution: Add fragrance oil only when the wax melts properly and just before you are ready to pour in the mold. Use more fragrance or use quality fragrance oils and candle wax.

The candle is not burning evenly
Reason: Wick may not be centered.
Solution: Make sure to secure the wick by using glue or wick centering equipment.

The flame is sputtering
Reason: Wax might contain water or air pockets that might have formed during the cooling of candles.
Solution: Make sure that no water drops get into the wax; fill the mold properly while pouring.

The candle is burning rapidly
Reasons: Air pockets might have formed around the wick, or wax is too soft for the wick.
Solution: Adjust the pouring temperature, release air pockets by tapping the sides of the container, or use hard wax or think wick.

Mottled effects on the candle surface

Reason: wax might contain excessive oil or the candle cooled very quickly.

Solution: Use little fragrance oil, use Vybar to prevent mottling, don't use excessive mold release spray, slow the cooling process by wrapping mold or container with a towel, or preheat the mold or container before you pour wax.

The candle does not burn

Reason: The wick has not been treated or wick is clogged Wick not primed   Wick may be clogged.

Solution: Used primed or treated wick. Don't use dyes that contain pigments that can clog the wick. Make sure the wax does not have dust or dirt.

Oil seeps from the candle

Reason: Perhaps too much fragrance oil has been used.

Solution: Check how much fragrance oil your wax can retain, use a little amount of fragrance oils. You can also use Vybar to increase fragrance oil retention.

Candle cracked while cooling down

Reason: You tried to cool the candle too quickly.

Solution: Don't place your candles in a fridge; let the candles cool in a warm environment.

Candle contains dye spots on the surface

Reason: Dye blocks or chips did not mix in the wax properly.

Solution: Use liquid dye and stir well. If you are using blocks or chips, allow it to melt well and then stir.

Candle color is fading
Reason: Perhaps you exposed the candles to UV lighting.
Solution: keep the candles away from direct sunlight. Use UV inhibitors for color retention.

The candle has a tunneling effect
Reason: Thin wick is used
Solution: Consider using a thick wick or soft wax

Tips

How to Center the Candle Wick
One of the common problems a candle maker experiences is an off-centered wick. If the wick is not centered, the candle will not burn properly, there will be too much melting, and uneven scent through.

You can center the wick by using a wick centering tool, wick bar, or self-centering wicks. These wick centering tools are easily available in the candle store online or offline. Attach one end of the wick on the wick centering tool and then place it inside the candle container. Hold the other end with a skewer while pouring wax.

You can also center the wick without using a wick centering tool. The easiest way to do this is by finding the center spot in your mold or container and then fixing the wick in the center. You can fix wick on the bottom of the container or mold by using a hot glue gun, glue dots or sticky tack.

You can also use a cored wick if you have a problem with centering.

How to Get Rid of Sinkholes in Candles

Another common problem while making candles is sinkholes. Sinkholes are the crater-like openings around the wick. Whether you are making container candles, pillar candles, or any kind of candles, sinkholes are very common.

Sinkholes appear in various sizes and depths and have adverse effects on your candles. Sinkholes occur during the cooling process. When you melt the wax, it expands, and when it cools down it shrinks. Sinkholes appear when the wax is shrinking during the cooling process.

This problem can be easily addressed. Let your candles take time to settle and cool down. Do not place your candles in the fridge and let the candle cool down in warm temperature.

When you see sinkholes being formed while pouring, you can fix this by re-pouring wax. Temperature is the key to candle making. You have to not only check the wax temperature but also the temperature of your workstation. The recommended room temperature is around 70 degrees F.

Make sure your candle cool downs normally. Using preheated molds or containers can also solve the sinkhole problem.

You should add dyes and fragrance only after the wax melts properly. When you are doing second poring, make sure there is at least a 2 hours' gap. You can also avoid sinkholes by pouring slowing. If you hurry, sinkholes will appear.

Certain types of waxes are more prone to sinkholes. Therefore, you have to choose candle wax wisely.

Thank you for reading this book, it was a pleasure to put it together. We have gone over the tools, the wax, wicks and the process of candle making. You are given some cool projects to try out and get familiar with the process.

Now it's your time to try out this new and exciting hobby! There are quite some new ideas and designs to discover!

If you have a few seconds of extra time, would you consider leaving some feedback for my book? As a self-publisher, your feedback is valuable and would help me get this book in front of more people.

Happy candle making!

Sandra. N

Notes

....

....

....

....

....

....

....

....

....

....

....

Printed in Great Britain
by Amazon